WALKING CLOSE

The RIVER ISE near KE

Number Thirteen in the popular series of walking guides

Contents

Walk		Miles	Page No
1	Cransley Reservoir	4½	4
2	Ise Triangle	6¼	6
3	Burton Wold	7¾	8
4	Round House	5	10
5	Clay Dick	7½	12
6	Furnace Lane	7¼	14
7	Lime Tree Avenue	4½	16
8	Twywell Hills and Dales	4½	18
9	Badsaddle Wood	6¾	20
10	Drayton Park	6	22

The walks contained in this booklet make use of rights of way, national recreational paths and riverside paths in the Kettering area. There is very little walking on roads except where unavoidable. Most are on firm, good quality paths and well marked and signposted. Paths may cross fields under cultivation and some are more obscure and less well directed; the detailed instructions will guide past these points. Some of the walks are in areas popular with walkers already, others are in areas less popular and perhaps less accessible.

Walked, Written and Drawn by Clive Brown

© Clive Brown 2003 - 2006
© 2nd Edition 2006 – 2012

Published by Clive Brown
ISBN 978-1-907669-13-2

PLEASE
Take care of the countryside
Your leisure is someone's livelihood

Close gates
Start no fires
Keep away from livestock and animals
Do not stray from marked paths
Take litter home
Do not damage walls, hedgerows or fences
Cross only at stiles or gates
Protect plants, trees and wildlife
Keep dogs on leads
Respect crops, machinery and rural property
Do not contaminate water

Although not essential we recommend good walking boots; during hot weather take something to drink on the way. All walks can easily be negotiated by an averagely fit person. The routes have been recently walked and surveyed, changes can however occur, please follow any signed diversions. Some paths cross fields which are under cultivation. All distances and times are approximate.

The maps give an accurate portrayal of the area, but scale has however been sacrificed in some cases for the sake of clarity and to fit restrictions of page size.

Walking Close To have taken every care in the research and production of this guide but cannot be held responsible for the safety of anyone using them.

During very wet weather, parts of these walks may become impassable through flooding, check before starting out. Stiles and rights of way can get overgrown during the summer; folding secateurs are a useful addition to a walker's rucksack.

Thanks to Angela for help in production of these booklets

Views or comments?
walkingcloseto@yahoo.co.uk

Reproduced from Ordnance Survey Mapping on behalf of The Controller of Her Majesty's Stationery Office. © Crown Copyright License No. 100037980.

Walking Close To the River Ise near Kettering

Kettering was known as Cytringan or Cytra's settlement in Saxon times. After the Norman Conquest it became part of the estate of the abbots of Peterborough; King Henry III granted a charter to hoid a market in Cateringe in 1227.

Geddington (walk no 5) has the best preserved of the three surviving Eleanor crosses. Eleanor of Castile married Edward I in 1254. It proved to be a happy match for a dynastically arranged marriage and the two were seldom apart. Eleanor died in Harby, Nottinghamshire, in November 1290. Her body was carried in solemn procession to Westminster abbey for internment. The funeral cortege stopped overnight on twelve occasions; Edward later had a cross erected at each of these locations in commemoration of his late wife. Geddington was well known to the royal couple as the site of a royal hunting lodge from the time of Henry II, Richard I and King John. The narrow packhorse bridge over the River Ise at Geddington dates from around 1250.

Wicksteed Park opened officially in 1921. Charles Wicksteed, a local industrialist, first purchased the land in 1913 with the intention of developing a model village for his growing engineering workforce. A trust was founded in 1916 to administer the funds and the estate. The company still produces and sells playground equipment.

Burton Latimer (walk no 3) is the home of the breakfast cereal Weetabix; it has been made here since 1932. The factory which produces 70 million biscuits each working week dominates the Ise valley below Kettering.

The Round House (walk no 4) was inscribed after a visit by the Duke of Wellington to Woodford House. Riding on Burton Wold (walk no 3) he remarked on the similarity of the surrounding landscape to the fields of Waterloo.

The Jay is the most colourful member of the crow family and is never very far away from deciduous woodland. It feeds mainly on acorns often hiding thousands in a secret cache. The flash of pinky-brown, black and white chequered wings and a noticeably white rump flying away will be preceded by a raucous screech.

We feel that it would be difficult to get lost with the instructions and map in this booklet, but recommend carrying an Ordnance Survey map. All walks are on Explorer Map No. 224; Landranger No. 141 covers at a smaller scale. Roads, geographical features and buildings, not on our map but visible from the walk can be easily identified

1   Cransley Reservoir

$4^1/_2$ Miles   2 Hours

Park in Great Cransley, no toilets, local pub the 'Three Cranes'.

1 Start from the crossroads; walk down Bridle Way (this is the road name, it becomes a bridleway). Follow it to the end and keep direction on the green bridleway to the gate (close to a mile). Go through, cross the field and the next stile. Continue under the disused railway, over the stile and along the left hand side of the field ahead. Maintain direction over two more stiles and over the next field which may be under cultivation but a track should be visible within the crop.
2 At the A14, turn left along the field edge with the hedge to the right; go over two stiles down a fenced track and over a footbridge.
3 Turn left across a stile and follow the stream to the field boundary, turn right this side of the hedge, walk up to and cross the stile to the left. Continue along the right hand side of the left hand field with the hedge to the right. Cross the stile at the top.
4 Walk up the road ahead signed Thorpe Malsor; turn left through a small gap in the hedge into the second field on the left. Carry on up the field edge parallel to the road. Nearly at the top corner, fork left and cross the field boundary next to a marker post. Keep direction over the next two fields.
5 At the junction, go straight on along Church Way. Turn left at the signpost just past the church, carry on through the kissing gate and round the double bend to the field boundary. Turn left down the right hand side of the field to the reservoir; bear left for a short way and then right over the dam. Bear right between the railings past the front of the clubhouse; continue through the kissing gate and up the left hand side of the field to the road.
6 Turn right past the farm, go over the old railway bridge and past the wood to a footpath sign on the left. Cross the stile and the field in the arrowed direction; go down the fenced track to Loddington road in Great Cransley. Turn left to the village centre and your vehicle.

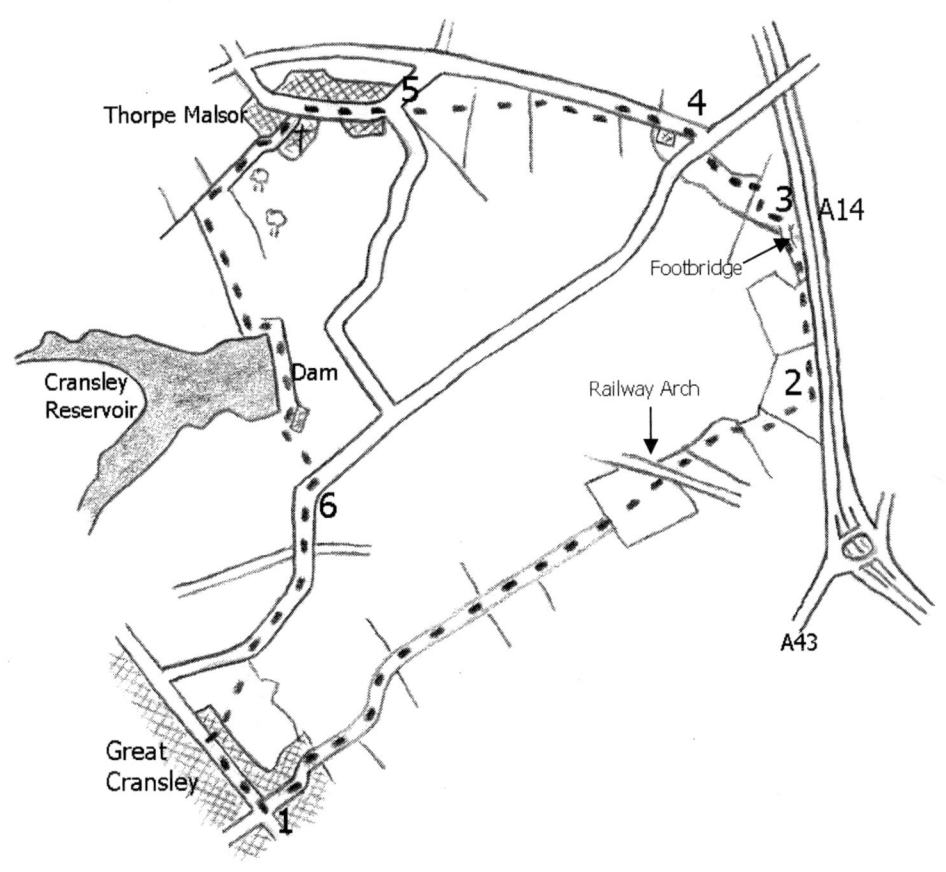

The Triangular Lodge near Rushton (walk no 2) was built under the instructions of Sir Thomas Tresham, an Elizabethan eccentric, who was regularly imprisoned during the reign of the first Elizabeth for his adherence to the Catholic faith. The design of the lodge echoes his belief in the Trinity. Sir Thomas died shortly before his son Sir Francis was caught up in the gunpowder plot; he died in the Tower before he could be executed.

2 Ise Triangle

$6^1/_4$ Miles $\qquad\qquad 2^3/_4$ Hours

Park in Rushton, no toilets, local pub the 'Thornhill Arms'

1 Start from the Thornhill Arms. Go down the High Street with the railings and parkland to the right, just around the left hand bend take the footpath signposted right. Pass through two gates between the house and the stable and across the stile. Turn right and walk over the footbridge crossing the Ise; take the arrowed direction and cross the stile at the top of the rise and carry on to the road.

2 Turn left along the road and right at the T-junction signposted Rothwell, follow this road for a mile and a quarter to just past the '30' signs. As the road turns left take the footpath to the right.

3 Cross the first field diagonally towards the telegraph pole, go over the dyke at the earth bridge and cut the corner of the next field this and several other fields on this walk may be under cultivation but paths should be visible within the crops. Cross a stile turn left and go over another stile close by; turn slight right and climb over the stile on the skyline. Keep direction to the next stile, cross this and the one to the left; continue on the left hand side of the field. Step over the stile at the gate and turn right along the field edge, turn left in the corner keep direction over the stile and go back over the river Ise by the footbridge.

4 Turn slightly to the right on the opposite bank and maintain direction over four stiles to the road; cross the road and the field beyond the track should be apparent within the crop.

5 Go over the railway carefully, high speed trains use this line. On the other side take a right hand diagonal across this vast field (track should be visible) to the top narrow corner. Go along the hardcore bridleway ahead; continue through the hedge gap and over the field to a hedge gap and footbridge in front of a telegraph pole halfway between the farm and the trees to the left. Turn left and follow the road to Pipewell.

6 Turn right at the T-junction, after 100yds, turn right up an obvious footpath (not signposted) and continue along the left hand side of two fields. Bear right through a gateway and keep direction on this grass bridleway for a mile and a quarter. Approaching Rushton it veers to the left over the railway bridge and down to Station Road opposite the Thornhill Arms.

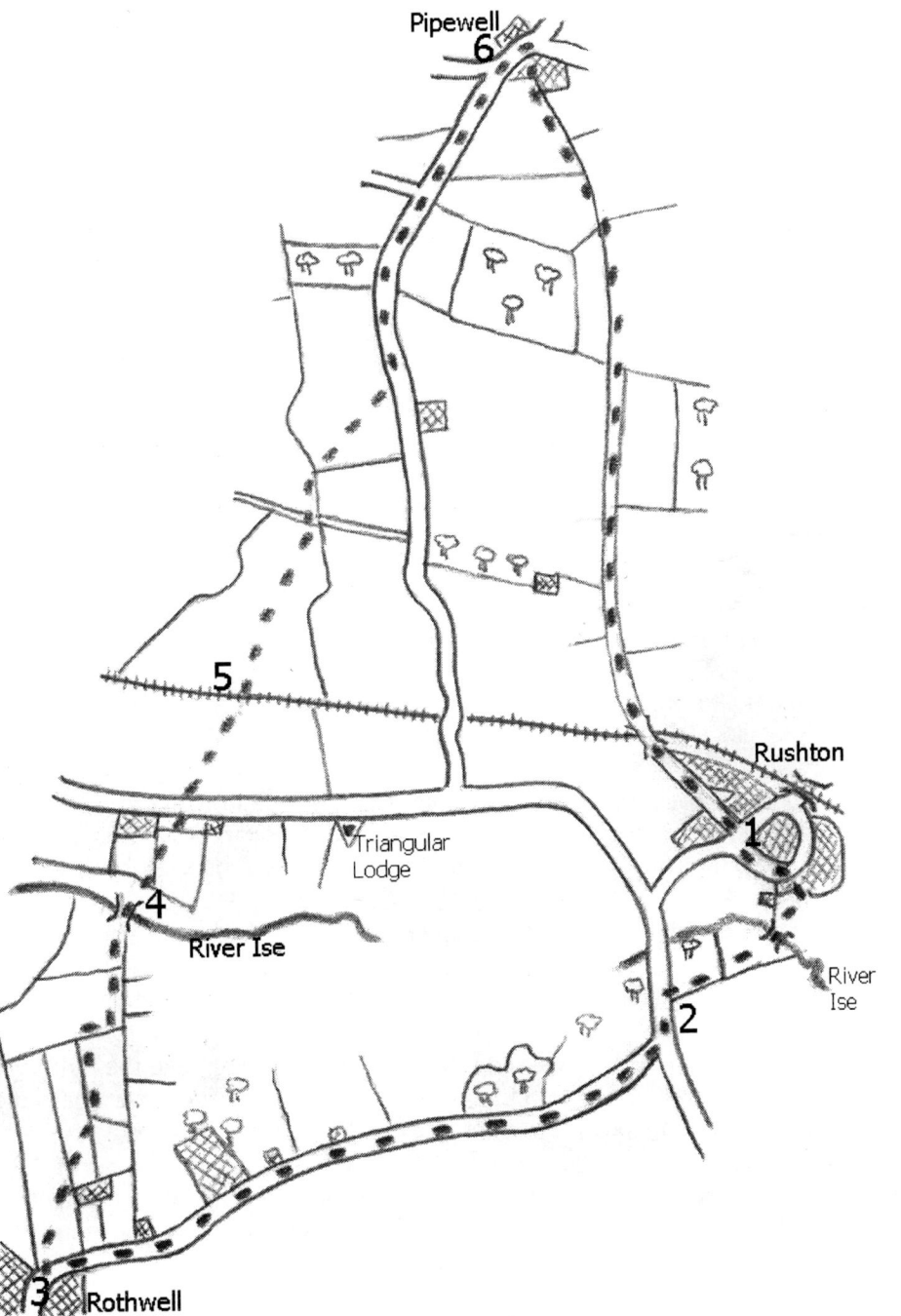

3   Burton Wold

7¾ Miles   3¾ Hours

Park in Burton Latimer in front of the 'Olde Victoria', off Church Street which is off High Street at the War Memorial; toilets, other pubs, cafés and takeaways in the town centre. The route crosses the busy A6 at point **2** and the return after point **9**. This walk may be muddy and take longer in wet weather, it is best in summer when the ground is hard.

1   Walk away from the town centre past the church; at the corner go straight on into Woodcock Street, down the right hand edge of the small piece of garden and over the stile. Take a slight diagonal right over the field and keep direction across the stile and a disused railway track. Cut across the corner of the field, go over the embankments via the stiles and the steps and carefully cross the busy A6.

2   From the stile at the top of the steps, take a right hand diagonal to the stile opposite, this field and several more ahead may be under cultivation but a track should be visible through any crops, cross and continue ahead. Maintain direction on the other side of the footbridge, go over another stile/footbridge and take a sharper angle right (direction arrowed) after the next footbridge to the far right corner of the field. Join the road to the left/straight on and carry on to the gate opposite the Round House at the A510.

3   Do not join the road, turn left 10yds from the field corner on a path gradually drawing left away from the road. Continue ahead over the farm road and the footbridge, cross the next footbridge, turn diagonally left and go straight on over the boundary.

4   Cross the dyke and turn left at the diversionary notice, follow the arrowed direction with the fence on the left, turn right at the sign and go up the slope between fence and hedge. Turn right at the corner and then left through the gate at the final diversion sign to the fence at the edge of the A14.

5   Turn left, follow the field edge and track parallel to the A14, take the farm road bearing left and then right, through the underpass. Go up the track over the cattle grid, bearing left to a signpost, turn right to the road.

6   Take the road right, past the junction, into Cranford St Johns; walk along the High Street to the path at the phone box. Turn left and keep ahead over the end of the road; cross the iron footbridge and take the path diagonally left across the field. Carry on through the gate, turn left at the road and fork left at the end.

<u>Completed on the next Page (Ten)</u>

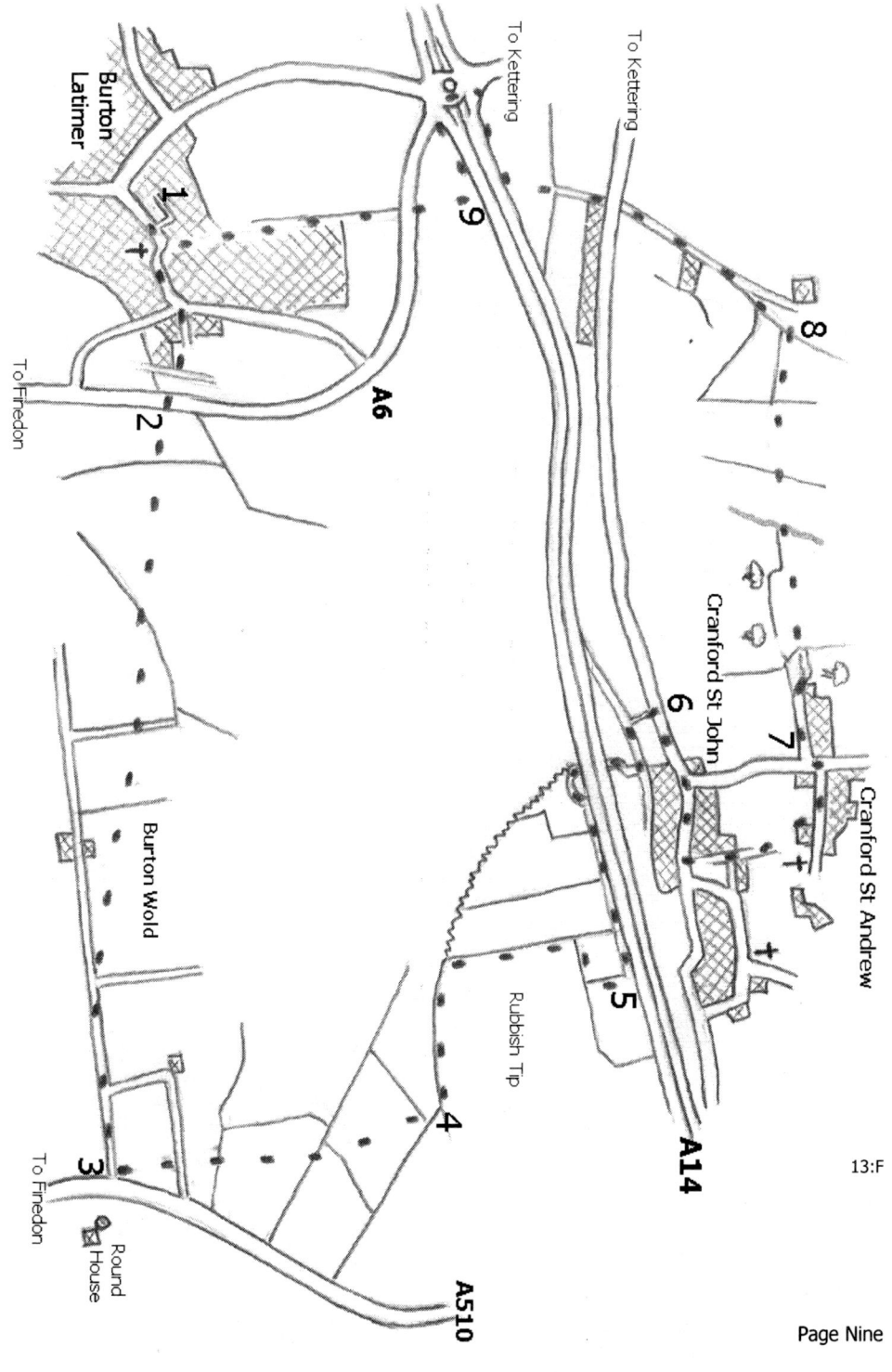

Completion of Burton Wold from Page Eight

7 Turn almost immediate right along Top Dysons and continue down the rough tarmac track at the end. Follow to the right then left through the gate and across the field parallel with the telegraph poles. Go over the footbridge, up the slope and past a marker post to the junction of paths.

8 Turn left, follow this tarmac bridleway to a road and cross carefully. Maintain direction down the signposted path next to the bungalow; through the trees on an obvious track and directly over the field to the A14. Turn right, walk parallel to the road, cross over at the flyover and follow the path on the right hand side of the westbound exit ramp to the stile.

9 Walk across this field at right angles, the path should be visible within any crop, to the stile and cross the A6 via the steps and the stile at the top. Keep direction along the right hand side of the fields and between the fence and houses, turn left for 20yds then back to the original direction down to Church Street. Turn right to the car park and your vehicle.

Round House Directions

1 Start facing the church, turn left and walk out of the village; join the main road left/straight on at the fork and follow the roadside path into Great Addington.

2 Carry on to the road junction in front of the church and turn left into Cranford Road. At the footpath signpost to Burton Latimer, turn left through the ornamental wrought iron gate and take the arrowed direction between hedges, which widen out after a gate on the left. As the hedge on the right ends take a right hand diagonal across the field to a gateway and marker post halfway along the opposite side; follow the farm road left, just before the road turns left, go over a stile on the right.

3 Turn left down the side of the field, carry on to the corner, go through the hedge gap and follow the arrowed direction over the field to the marker post. Walk along the edge of the field through the farmyard to the left of Round House, to the signpost almost at the road (the A510).

4 Turn sharp left taking a diagonal away from the road, across the field close to the telegraph pole through a narrow hedge gap and over the next two fields where the marker posts are more visible, these fields may again be under cultivation. Bear right at the marker post at the boundary at the top of the rise and keep the arrowed direction with Poplar Farm, the barn and the hedge all on the left. Join the road to the right for 30yds then resume direction across the field to stile in the far corner.

5 Walk along the road for 40yds and turn left at the bridleway sign. Follow this tarmac bridleway for half a mile and turn left with it before the dyke at the bottom of the dip is reached. Continue through a double bend, past a large pond and bear right uphill and then down the slope into Little Addington and your vehicle.

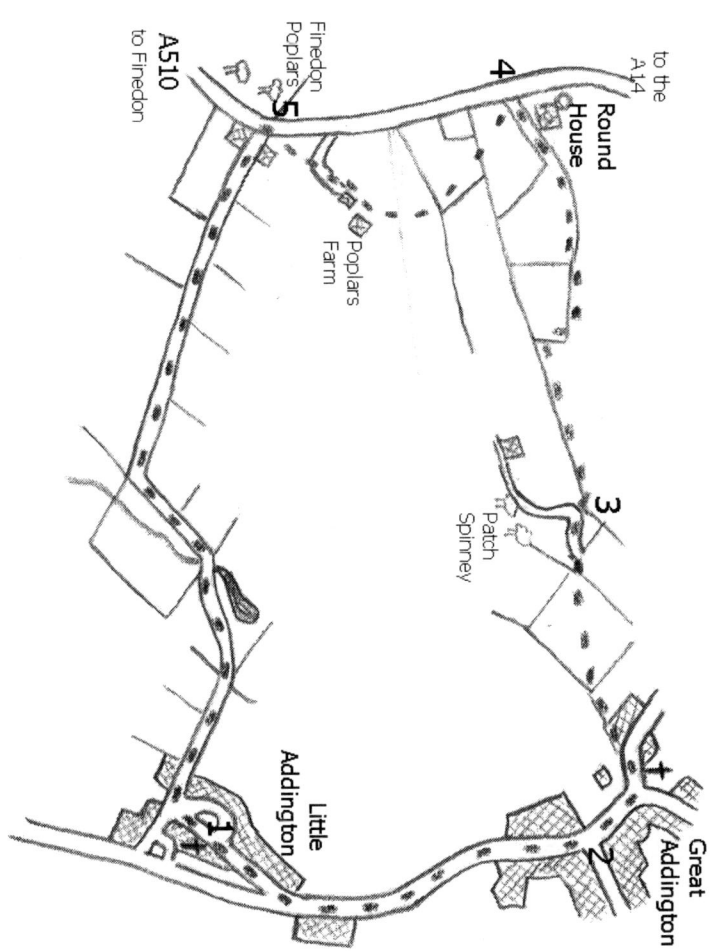

4   Round House

5 Miles   2 Hours

Find a parking space in Little Addington. No toilets, local pub the 'Bell'

5   Clay Dick

7½ Miles   3½ to 4 Hours

Park in Geddington, no toilets, local pubs the 'White Hart' and the 'Star Inn'. A tough walk in wet weather, the first half particularly can be very muddy.

1   Start from the cross; facing the church turn right along Grafton Road and left into West Street. Go past the school and Chase Farm; turn right up the steps close to the lamppost between nos 2 and 4. Go down the walled path and over the stile, keep to the right hand side of the field and go over the next stile.

2   Take a left hand diagonal across the first of several fields which may be under cultivation, the tracks however should be visible within any crops, to a stile to the left of the upright concrete pipe. Maintain direction over the next field, cross the footbridge and turn slight right towards the corner of the wood ahead.

3 Continue, past the rusting tank, roughly parallel to and 40yds away from the wood, cross the footbridge/stile and walk ahead down the hardcore bridleway. As the bridleway turns right carry on ahead past the marker post, across another cultivated field and through the hedge gap to next marker post. Keep direction down the right hand side of the field past another rusty tank on stilts; turn left in the corner and right through the gateway 40yds on.

4 Go straight across the first field and slightly right at the next (note marker posts at boundaries) midway between pylons, go not through the wide gap but over the almost hidden stile to the left of it. Cross to the middle corner (see map), step over the stile to the left and take a right hand diagonal to the stile at the bottom end.

5 Cross and follow the left hand field edge with the hedge and the fence to the left, continue down the left hand side of the next field and go over the stile. Turn right and walk around the wandering boundary of this field, cross the stile to the right at the end and walk down the left hand field edge go over the stile to the left just before the gate. Keep direction over two more stiles and along a narrow overgrown path to the road in Brigstock.

6 Turn left, past the end of Bridge Street, which leads to the village centre and carry on ahead down Dusthill Road. This road continues to Chase Farm where it becomes a rutted grass bridleway called Clay Dick, keep going on this track past the transmitter aeriel and along the edge of Geddington Chase, for two miles to a metal barrier at a T-junction.

7 Go down the track to the left, which runs into Geddington, along West Street, to find your vehicle.

6   Furnace Lane

7$^1/_4$ Miles   3 Hours

Park in Pytchley, no toilets, local pub the 'Overstone Arms'. Muddy in wet weather.

1   Start from the top of Butcher's Lane, next to the school. Walk down the Lane past the school entrance; carry straight on along the path between the house and the wall. Cross two stiles and take a left hand diagonal to a stile to the right of the houses, step over the stile and turn right down the road.

2   Turn left at the signpost at the bottom of the dip, cross the stile and turn right at a shallow angle away from the fence to a triple stile/footbridge to the left of the barn. Keep direction to the bottom left corner step over the stile and turn left through the trees, follow the arrowed direction on the marker post over the field which may be under cultivation but a track is normally visible through it.

3   From the marker post at the corner continue through the hedge gap and along the right hand side of the field, turn right through a hedge gap and left back to the original direction, hedge now on the left, up to the road.

4   Keep direction over the road and across the field, farm buildings to the right, a track should be visible within any crop, cross the footbridge, the path goes straight on here but if there is a crop in the field it may be easier to walk around the edge. Walk between the fences and turn right over the stile into the school playing field, carry on down the right hand edge and turn left at the kissing gate. Go through the next kissing gate and down between the school and the church to the road.

5   Turn left and walk out of the village of Little Harrowden on the B574 to the crossroads at the A509. Cross straight over into Furnace Lane, continue downhill and under the railway, turn left with the road, past the factories to the T-junction.

6   Keep going straight ahead over the stile, keep to the right, turn right through the second gate and turn left to continue direction with the hedge to the left. Cross the concrete bridge into the next field, carry on over the stile in the corner; go over the field to the brick and latticework footbridge (not the wider bridge near left) and cross the railway.

7   Continue over the concrete ladder stile, take a right hand diagonal across the corner of the field and keep direction to a stile. Go down the short grass path into Isham, turn left and follow the street up to the Kettering Road at the church (the A509). Turn right, walk through the village and turn left at the footpath just before the cemetery signposted Pytchley.

Completed on the next Page (Sixteen)

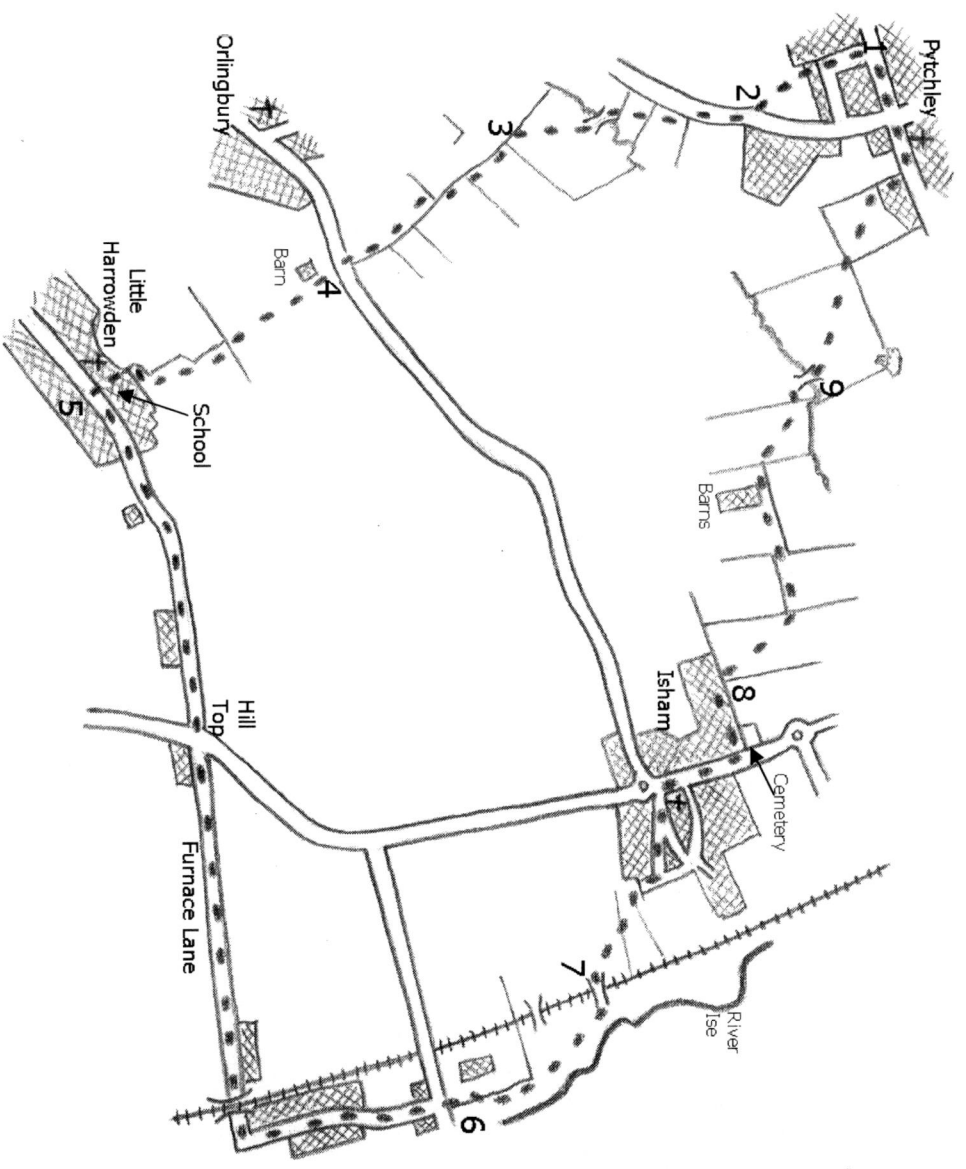

Completion of 6 Furnace Lane from Page Fourteen

8   Turn right over the stile and cross the field left at a 45° angle to the stile marked by a tall yellow topped post, cross the stile and carry on along the left hand field edge. Go over the next stile and continue with the hedge now on the right. Continue over the wobbly stile in the corner take a right hand diagonal (the track should be visible within the crop) to a stile to the left of the field corner. Cross, turn right, then left in the corner and follow the right hand edge of the field with the stream on the right to the footbridge.

9   Cross the footbridge, keep direction, heading to just left of the church tower, through this field over the stile and the next field. In the top left hand corner to the left of the big house, go down the short enclosed track, through the gate and along the left hand side of the field to the road. Turn left into the village and your vehicle.

---

7   Lime Tree Avenue

$4^1/_2$ Miles $2^1/_2$ Hours

Find a parking space in Grafton Underwood, no toilets, no refreshments. **This walk will be very muddy when wet.**

1   Start from the double footpath sign in the village centre, cross the stream and walk west down the wide stone track between the houses. Go through the smaller of the two wooden gates and up to the top of the narrow field. Continue Through the gate at the top right and along the left hand side of the field beyond. Cross the stile in the corner and the next 20yds to the right.

2   Turn left down the field edge; go through the boundary and cross the field diagonally to the gate in the corner. Turn left, walk 400yds and turn down the green bridleway signed to the right.

3   Maintain direction to the end of the third field and turn right in front of the concrete bollards; follow the field edge with the hedge to the left. Turn right for 60yds, at the corner at the bottom of the dip; then left across the dyke.

4   Continue direction along the edge of this field and the next with the hedge to the right. Go across the field ahead at a slight diagonal right, the track in this field should be visible through any crop. Through the gate take a slight diagonal left and keep direction through two fields to the road corner. Carry on left/ahead to the edge of Warkton.

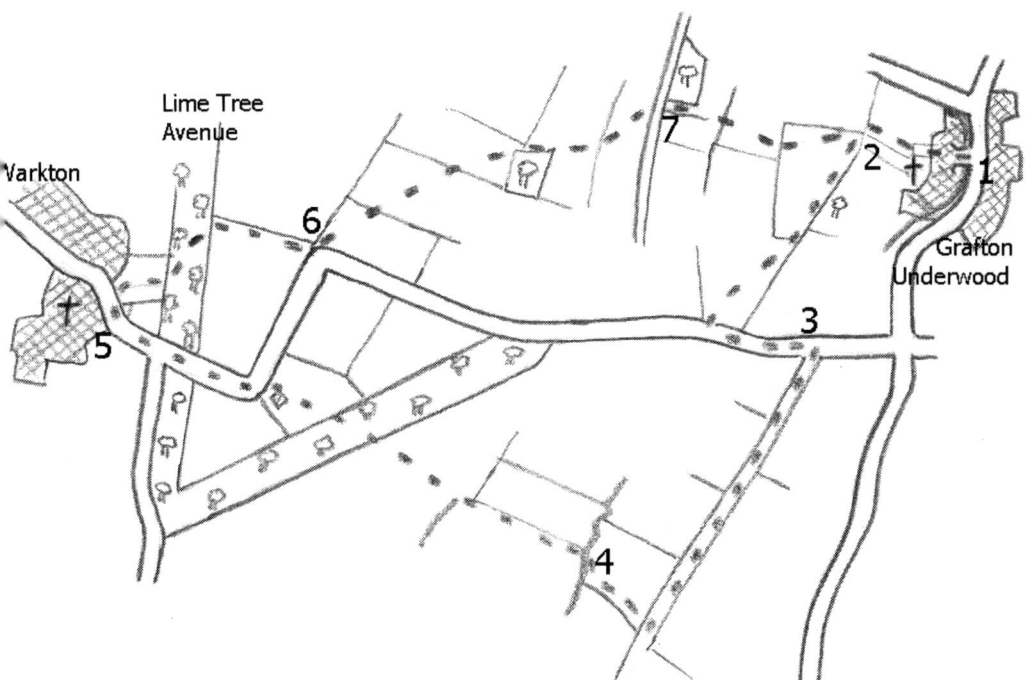

5 Turn right before the first pair of houses down a stony drive, go over the stile up the slope and along the enclosed path bearing right to another stile. Cross and walk on a left hand diagonal through the trees of Lime Tree Avenue to a stile on the other side. Step over this stile and walk along the left hand side of the field and across the stile in the corner.

6 Take a shallow diagonal left to a stile, cross and keep direction across this field, track should be visible, turn to a slightly sharper angle to the right over the next field over the footbridge, through the corner and bear right along the right hand field edge, pond and trees to the right. Keep straight on at the corner over the field and the footbridge; go through the hedge gap and take a left hand diagonal to the gap in front of the conifers and cross the hardcore farm road.

7 Go down the left hand side of the field with the conifers to the left, maintain direction through the hedge gap and over the next field. Continue through another hedge gap slightly left to the top left corner, cross a stile and the next 20yds left and join the outward route back to Grafton Underwood and your vehicle.

The 2nd **Duke of Montagu** planted many miles of elm and lime tree avenues around the Boughton area during the early 18th Century; he gained the nickname of 'John the Planter'. The dukedom became extinct when he died in 1749.

8 Twywell Hills and Dales

4$^{1}/_{2}$ Miles   2 Hours

Park in the Twywell Hills and Dales car park north of the junction of the A14 with the A510, east of Kettering. No toilets, no facilities.

1 Walk from the information board to the left and go through the little gate at the end of the stony path and turn left. Carry on between the marker post and the next information board and turn left through the gate in the left hand corner. Follow the left hand edge of the right hand field to the corner, cross the stile/footbridge and continue past the right hand end of the pond. Turn left to a stile in the fence and cross, bear left and carry on with the stream on the left. Go through the gate and down the lane past the sewage works. Pass through the small gate and turn right.
2 Follow the road uphill, as it swings left, take the direction of the signpost across the field to the far corner, this field may be under cultivation but a track is normally visible. Turn slight left down the right hand side of the field edge with the hedge on the right; go through the hedge gap to the right of the small stand of trees. Turn right at the second marker post along the right hand edge of the left hand field.
3 Cross the footbridge in the corner and turn left, at the next boundary take a right hand diagonal from the marker post to the opposite side; turn left and walk past the footbridge to the field corner. Turn to the right through the gateway and along the left hand field side; halfway down turn left at the metal post and carry on up the left hand of the right hand field to the road.
4 Turn right; as the road bends right go straight on through the gate and cross the field diagonally right to the stile to the right of the cottage that juts out into the field. At the end of the enclosed path turn left along the street through Twywell.
5 Towards the end of the village go right/straight on down The Lane, signposted to the Hills and Dales. Turn right in front of the marker post, go through the kissing gate and follow the left hand side of the field. Through the next kissing gate go down the steps and turn right to the kissing gate in the woodland ahead.
6 Pass through into Twywell Hills and Dales and go up the steps to the signpost; turn right to the marker post at the top of the rise and then left along the ridge. Keep direction making a short detour to the left then back at the red arrow markers. (This last section when the end appears to be close seems to take ages.) Bear right finally uphill, go through the kissing gate; turn left to the car park and your vehicle.

13:F

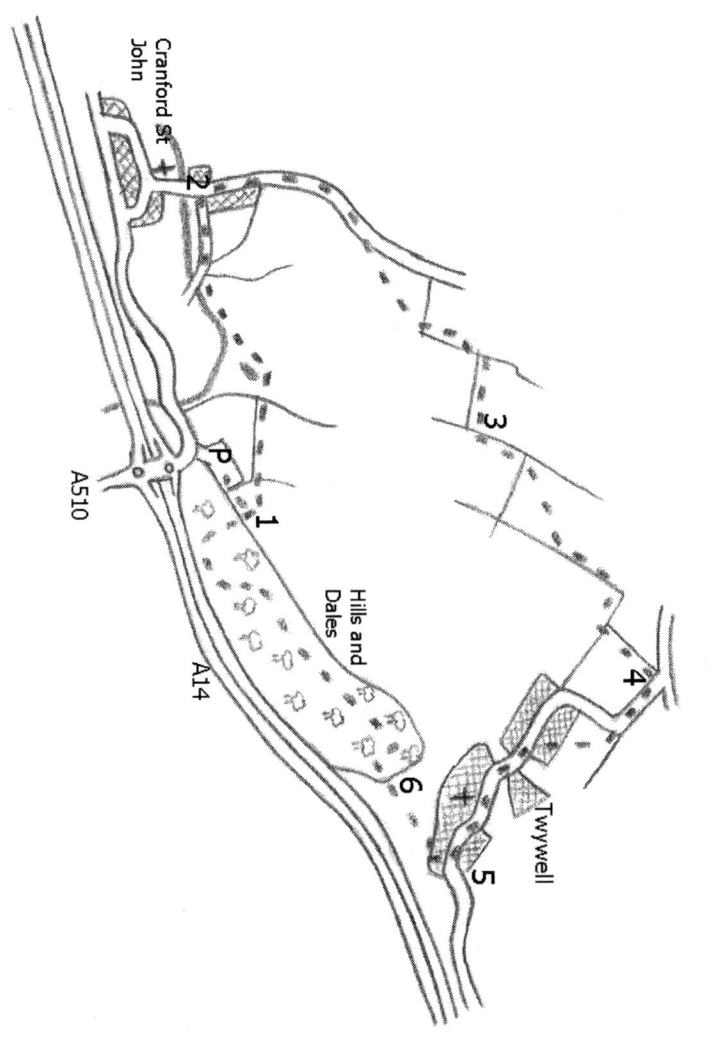

The distinctive contours of Twywell Hills and Dales were formed during the extraction of iron ore. Massive trenches were dug, the ore was taken out and then the waste from the next trench used to refill them. Local names, such as Furnace Lane (walk no 6) reflect the area's connections with the iron industry.

9   Badsaddle Wood

6³/₄ Miles   3 Hours

Park in Broughton pubs and shops locally, no toilets. **Very muddy when wet.**

1 Start from the High Street, walk out of Broughton on Northampton Road. Turn left through the gate at the signpost opposite the garage. Cross the short stretch of field to the hedge corner, this and several other fields on this walk may be under cultivation, paths should be visible within any crops. Continue ahead with the hedge to the left to a stile on the left, cross and keep original direction with the hedge now to the right. Cross the first footbridge and then the next over the deeper stream.

2 Turn right through the hedge gap and cross the field on a left hand diagonal to the gate in the opposite corner. Go over the road, carry on ahead along the farm road and keep to the road on the right past the farm.

3 After 400yds turn right at an arrow marker. Cross the field and the next over the boundary (tracks should be visible), continue over the footbridge and head for the road to the left of Badsaddle Farm ahead; turn right with the road around the farm and then left into a grass bridleway to the right of Badsaddle Wood.

4 At the A43, turn left and go through the lay-by, a short distance beyond turn left at a signpost through a hedge gap. Go down the right hand side of the field, through the wide hedge gap, turn diagonally left to the opposite corner and carry on along the farm track. Go over the more substantial farm road, close to a pylon and down the left hand side of the field ahead with the trees to the left.

5 At the bottom of the slope turn right for 30yds and then cross a sizeable footbridge to get back to the original direction with the trees on the left, keep direction along an enclosed bridleway and across the road.

6 Cross the field ahead at a slight diagonal left to the hedge corner and continue ahead with the hedge to the left, go through the gateways into the next field. Walk over this field moving left away from the right hand edge through the dip and a line of trees to a gate. Cross the this field at a slight diagonal left to the gateway/hedge gap and carry on through another gate to a stile just past some farm buildings.

7 Turn left through a small farmyard and down the path between the house and the wall, keep straight on, into Pytchley along Butcher's Lane to High Street and turn left. Fork right into Top End, go to the end and turn left through a small farmyard. Turn right past a black barn to follow a bridleway past more farm buildings and out between fields. This enclosed bridleway bears left to a wide hedge gap; bear right across the field corner, go through the hedge gap and then follow the right hand edge of the field with the trees to the right.

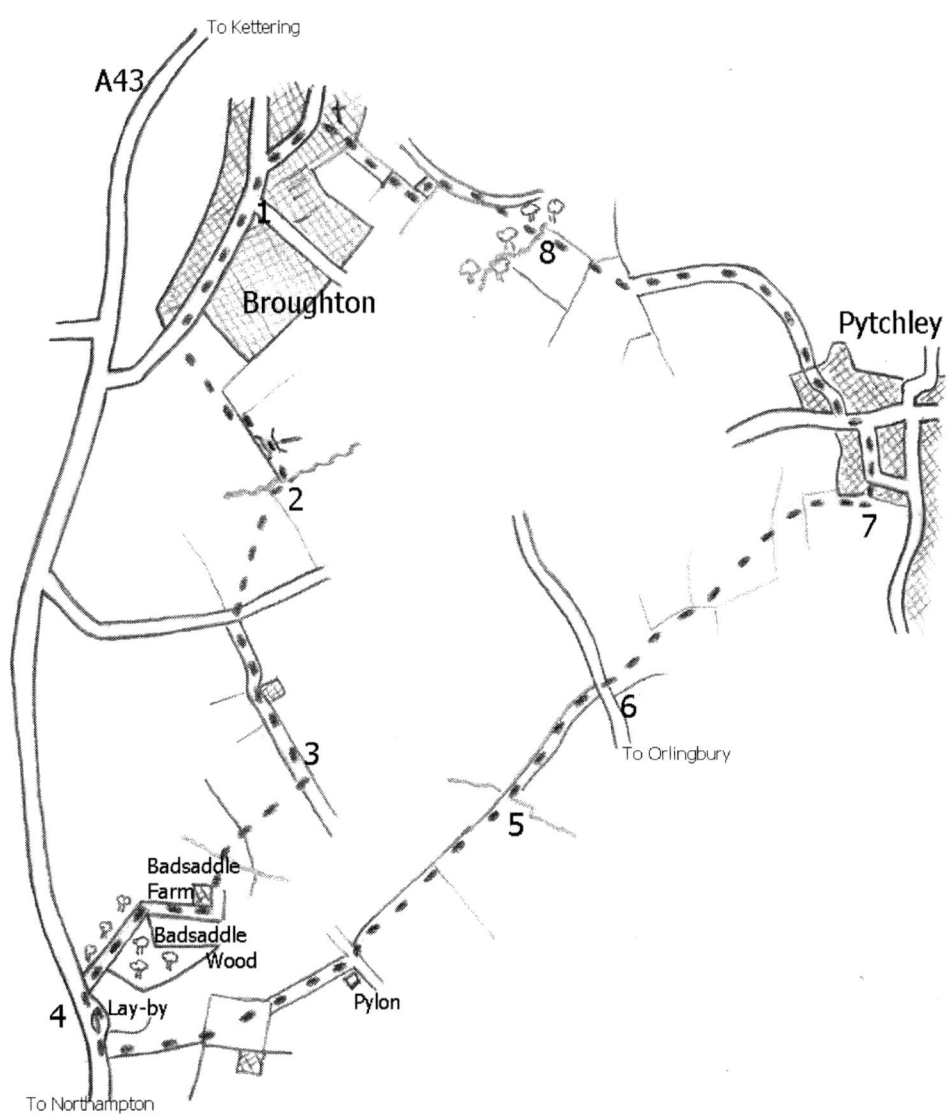

8 Drop down with the track into Underwood's Hill Spinney, cross the footbridge and join the bridleway to the right at the top of the slope. Go through a gate and turn left over a stile down a narrow overgrown path; turn right after the concrete stile at the other end. Continue over another stile and along an enclosed path; cross the next stile, carry on between walls through what appears to be a private yard and out of a passage flanked by a house and an outhouse. Walk down the path to Church Street and turn left into Broughton to find your vehicle.

10   Drayton Park

6 Miles $2^1/_2$ Hours

Find a parking space in Lowick, no toilets.

1 Leave the village along Drayton Road, continue over the cattle grid, through the Drayton Estate and turn right at the junction at Drayton House. Follow the road left and right, turn left at the marker discs on the gatepost and continue along the road past the 'No Through Road' sign.

2 Just past the two houses turn right at the junction and bear left along the gravelly farm track at Home Farm. Carry on around the double bends to the bottom of the slope. Turn left for 30yds and then right uphill between the fence and the churchyard, continue along the path to the road in Slipton village. Turn left; bear left at the junction and walk up to the footpath signpost. Turn right up the driveway; go through the wide and then the narrow gate.

3 Keep direction over the stile and carry on through the gate in the right hand corner of the next field. Turn immediate left over the gate, bear right and continue with Manor Farm to the right, go through the metal gate by the telegraph pole, bear left and step over the stile at the end. Continue along the wide track between trees, cross the stile and go past the pub, bear right over a stile and on to the road.

4 Turn left, follow the road out of Twywell village and carry on for nearly a mile to the staggered crossroads. Take the road left towards Slipton and continue straight on past the concrete block, up the hedged bridleway.

5 After 800yds turn right at an easily missed gatepost marked by discs, turn immediate left along the field edge with the hedge to the left. As this edge bears left, go straight on over the field which may be under cultivation although a path should be well marked and go through the gate at the top corner (it may be easier to go around the field edge). Maintain direction over the farm road along the hardcore track between hedges and trees.

6 As this track turns left, keep straight on down the right hand field edge and bear left at the marker post. Turn right at the next marker post over the sunken farm road and cross the field (a track should be visible), carry on along the field edge and follow it to the right. Cross over the footbridge and bear left across the field past the corner of the wall to the signpost at the road. Turn left, back into Lowick village to find your vehicle.

13:F

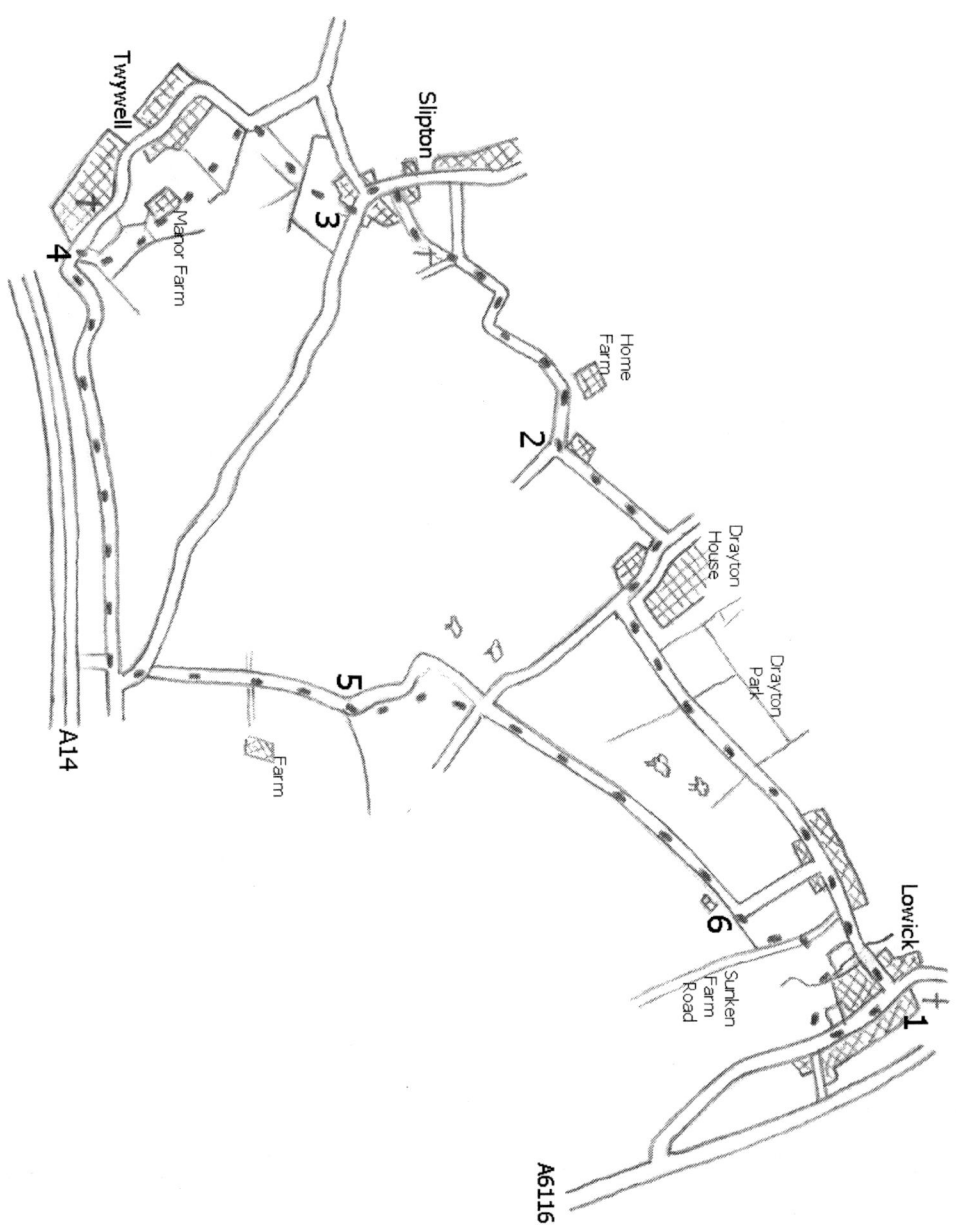

The 'Walking Close to' Series

Peterborough
The Nene near Peterborough
The Nene Valley Railway near Wansford
The Nene near Oundle
The Torpel Way (Peterborough to Stamford)
The Great North Road near Stilton

Cambridge
Grafham Water (Huntingdonshire)
The Great Ouse in Huntingdonshire
The Cam and the Granta near Cambridge
Newmarket
The Isle of Ely

Northamptonshire/Warwickshire
The Nene near Thrapston
The Nene near Wellingborough
The River Ise near Kettering
The Nene near Northampton
Pitsford Water
Rockingham Forest
Daventry and North West Northamptonshire
Rugby

Leicestershire
Rutland Water
Eye Brook near Uppingham
The Soar near Leicester
Lutterworth
The Vale of Belvoir (North Leicestershire)
Melton Mowbray
The Welland near Market Harborough

Lincolnshire
The Welland near Stamford
Bourne and the Deepings
South Lincolnshire

Suffolk
Lavenham in Suffolk
Bury St Edmunds
The Stour near Sudbury
The Orwell near Ipswich
Dedham Vale
Stowmarket
Clare, Cavendish and Haverhill

Berkshire
The River Pang (Reading/Newbury)

Essex/Hertfordshire
Hertford and the Lee Valley
The Colne near Colchester
Epping Forest (North London)
Chelmsford
Saffron Walden (2012)

Wiltshire/Bath
The Avon near Bath
Bradford-on-Avon
Corsham and Box
The Avon near Chippenham

Bedfordshire/Milton Keynes
The Great Ouse near Bedford
The Great Ouse North of Milton Keynes
Woburn Abbey

Somerset & Devon
Cheddar Gorge
Glastonbury and the City of Wells
The Quantock Hills
The East Devon Coast (Sidmouth, Branscombe and Beer)
Exmouth and East Devon

Norfolk
The Norfolk Broads (Northern Area)
The Norfolk Broads (Southern Area)
The Great Ouse near King's Lynn
North West Norfolk (Hunstanton and Wells)
Thetford Forest
North Norfolk (Cromer and Sheringham)

Nottinghamshire
Sherwood Forest
The Dukeries (Sherwood Forest)
The Trent near Nottingham

Oxfordshire
The Thames near Oxford
The Cotswolds near Witney
The Vale of White Horse
Woodstock and Blenheim Palace
Henley-on-Thames
Banbury

Cumbria
Cartmel and Southern Lakeland

Hereford and Worcester
The Severn near Worcester
South West Herefordshire (Hay-on-Wye and Kington)
The Malvern Hills